Citrus

by Ethel and Georgeanne Brennan

collages by Ann Field

CHRONICLE BOOKS

SAN FRANCISCO

Library of Congress Cataloging-in-Publication Data:

Brennan, Georgeanne, 1943-
     Citrus / Georgeanne Brennan and Ethel Brennan;
     illustrations by Ann Field
         p. cm.
     Includes index.
     ISBN 0-8118-0602-2
     1. cookery (Citrus fruits) I. Brennan, Ethel. II. Title.
TX813.C5B73 1995
641.6'4304 — dc20   94-40920 CIP

Book and cover design by Gretchen Scoble
with Anne Shannon and Pamela Geismar

Collages photographed by Holly Lindem

Printed in Hong Kong.

Distributed in Canada by Raincoast Books, 8680 Cambie St., Vancouver, B.C. V6P 6M9

10 9 8 7 6 5 4 3 2 1

Chronicle Books
275 Fifth Street
San Francisco, CA 94103

Acknowledgments

We would like to thank
Leslie Jonath, Bill LeBlond, Susan Lescher,
Sharon Silva, and Kerri Pollard
for their help and support.

Table of Contents

Introduction

Citrus fruits have enjoyed a colorful and tumultuous journey around the world since leaving their native lands in India, China, and areas of Southeast Asia. Travelers and adventurers returning to Europe from the far reaches of Asia along the Silk Road around 300 B.C. brought home with them exotic seeds of the fragrant citron, a large lemon-shaped fruit. Later, in the first and second centuries A.D., along the same trade route linking the Roman Empire to the East, the seeds of lemons, oranges, and mandarins were carried to southern Europe. Elaborate gardens and greenhouses were built to house the exotic fruit trees, which were commonly referred to as Persian apples or golden balls, and were coveted primarily for their beauty.

But long before citrus fruits became fixtures in the empires of the Greeks and Romans, they were intricately woven into the cultural and religious traditions of their eastern homelands. The delicate but powerful fragrance emitted from the leaves, flowers, and fruits, especially of the citron and the large, grapefruit-shaped pomelo, encouraged their use in a variety of ceremonial and religious rituals. Even today in areas of China, newborn babies are still bathed in water floating with the leaves and blossoms of the pomelo to wash away any impurities they may be carrying into their new world. During the Chinese New Year, the same ritual is performed on small children to cleanse them for the upcoming twelve months. The conquering of Babylon introduced the citron to the Jews. They called the fruit *etrog,* and now, during the Feast of the Tabernacles, the large, greenish-yellow, knobby-surfaced fruits are tied to cut branches of palm, willow, and myrtle and carried to synagogues.

Oranges have been given as gifts for millennia. Around 2200 B.C. a pomelo and an orange wrapped in hand-embroidered silk were presented as a tribute to the Chinese emperor, Tayun. Europe embraced the beautiful fruits, which were presented as tokens of appreciation by the ancient Greeks. Henry IV gave his mother-in-law, Catherine de Medici, an orangerie (greenhouse) for her Tuileries Palace in Paris (although she never lived there to enjoy it). Farther north, across the icy English channel, British parents have long tucked fresh oranges into their children's Christmas stockings.

By the fifteenth century, citrus fruits had become common fixtures throughout Europe, and it was not long before they spread across the Americas as well. Citrus first reached the New World with the second voyage of Christopher Columbus in 1493. The explorer brought with him the seeds of lemons, sweet oranges, sour oranges, and citrons, all of which were planted on the island of Hispanola. The warm Caribbean climate enabled the fruits to flourish there. Some two hundred years later, an Englishman, Captain Shaddock, brought the first pomelos to the West Indies, having carried them from his travels in the South Pacific. The fruits, the largest of the citrus family, are still sometimes called shaddocks after the captain. Shortly after the pomelo reached the Caribbean, a smaller and sweeter mutation (or possibly hybrid) evolved and it became known as the grapefruit.

The Portuguese also played an important role in the travels of citrus. They sailed the high seas of Asia and the New World in pursuit of treasures and territory and eventually brought back to Brazil a delicious variety of sweet orange, which is thought to have mutated into the navel orange, now the most commonly grown commercial sweet orange in California.

Anatomy of Citrus

Each element that makes up a citrus fruit can be used in cooking: the outer rind, or zest; the inner white rind; the inner fruit, called the pulp; and the juice. Each of these components is a source of inspiration to the culinary spirit. On a commercial level, the makeup of citrus fruits is mined even further, with the essential oils used in the pharmaceutical and cosmetic industries. Citrus blossoms, especially those of oranges, are widely used in the perfume industry.

The zest contains essential oils that add a subtle yet lively layering of flavors to many dishes. It can be grated from the whole fruit on the small holes of a hand-held grater, gently removed using a vegetable peeler or a sharp paring knife, or peeled off in long, thin shreds with a special tool called a citrus zester. When preparing zest, it is important to remove only the outer colored portion of the rind, as the white, spongy part that lies beneath it is bitter. Zest can be used as a garnish or tossed into sauces, cake batters, salads, and dressings.

The inner rind provides a rich source of pectin, making this part of the fruit a useful ingredient for all types of jams, jellies, and confections. Leave the outer and inner rind intact when cooking dishes that require extra or natural pectin. On its own, the inner rind is bitter. Some fruits, such as the pomelo and grapefruit, have a very thick inner rind, which can be trimmed down. Try adding a tablespoon or two of finely chopped inner rind (with outer rind) to a favorite blackberry or apricot jam recipe. The citron, although seldom found fresh, has a thick inner rind, and is widely used to make commercial candied rind.

The pulp is the meat of the citrus fruit. It is most commonly used by sectioning it or extracting its juices. A protective membrane covers each section of the pulp, and in some fruits, such as the pomelo, it is tough or unattractive and should be removed before adding

LEMON

the pulp to a dish. To remove, peel away the outer rind and as much of the inner rind as possible from the fruit. Then using a small paring knife, trim away the protective membrane by cutting along the sides of the sections, thereby freeing them.

The juice is generally extracted from the fruit with a citrus reamer, a ribbed, cone-shaped tool that releases the juice when the cut fruit is pressed down and rotated atop the cone. Both manual and electric reamers are available. Sometimes the pulp is blended with the extracted juice to make a thicker consistency; other times, the juice is strained through a sieve lined with cheesecloth to remove all traces of the pulp. How you treat the juice will depend upon the individual recipe. Most citrus fruits are not seedless, and it is important to remove the tiny pips when using the pulp or the juice.

Finally, there is the grape-sized kumquat and its hybrid offspring, the orangequat and the limequat. For these, it is not necessary to remove the bitter membrane or strain out the seeds. Indeed, this family is unique in the citrus world, for its members are eaten rind and all.

When cooking with citrus fruits, it is sometimes necessary to use nonreactive pans and oven utensils, that is, to avoid cast iron and aluminum. The acid in the juice can adversely react with these metals, causing the flavor and color of a dish to change. This is especially important when citrus is a primary ingredient used for deglazing, for making sauces, or when whole sections are being sautéed. If using zest or juice in small quantities for flavoring, it is not critical to use nonreactive utensils.

Oranges

Sirloin Strips Sautéed with Orange Juice *20*

Chicken Wings with Orange-Mustard Glaze *21*

Blood Oranges, Anchovies, and Salt-Cured Olives *22*

Pork Brochettes Marinated in Orange Sauce *24*

Salad of Sweet Oranges, Endive, and Sugared Walnuts *25*

Bread Pudding with Sweet Oranges *26*

Spicy Marinade with Orange *27*

Citrus Salsa *28*

Custard Tart of Strawberries and Oranges *30*

Savory Galettes of Sweet Potato and Orange *33*

Sherbert-Filled Oranges *34*

Bread Salad with Orange and Arugula *36*

$\mathcal{O}$ranges fall into two general categories: sweet and sour. Among the best known of the sweet oranges is the navel orange, which is seedless and has a small secondary orange growing at its blossom end. The protuberance looks much like a navel, thus the name. Another popular sweet orange is the Valencia, a fruit highly valued for its abundant juice and near-seedless oblong segments.

Sour oranges are descended from wild oranges that were first domesticated for ornamental purposes. Their powerful aromatic qualities make up for the intense bitter flavor. The Bouquet des Fleures variety is important in the perfume industry for its fragrant blossoms and essential oils. In Spain, between the outskirts of the southwestern riverbank city of Seville and the coast of the Atlantic Ocean near the Strait of Gibraltar, sprawl acres of small commercial orange trees that seem to tumble against the beaches. These are the treasured sour Seville oranges, favored in England for the making of marmalade.

Not far from these Spanish orchards lies the hot, dry coastline of North Africa. This region, along with Spain, Sicily, and Israel, provides many of Europe's oranges, including the exquisite, sweet blood orange. Its interior coloring can vary from pale pinkish orange to deep magenta and its flavor is sweet and berrylike. For years my family referred to blood oranges as Algerian or Moroccan oranges because we associated them with the Algerian migrant workers who harvested the vineyards around our home in Provence. As we worked alongside them, we would chat with the Algerian men, who smoked Turkish tobacco and offered us treats of these distinctive oranges.

Sirloin

STRIPS SAUTÉED WITH ORANGE JUICE

Adapted from a dish that celebrates the orchards of the orange trees
that dot the Spanish landscape, this simple preparation has a rich sauce
that is perfect spooned over a mound of fluffy white rice.

1 cup strained fresh orange juice
(about 3 oranges)

1 tablespoon finely grated orange
zest (about 1 orange)

2 garlic cloves, minced

½ teaspoon salt

½ teaspoon freshly ground
black pepper

2 tablespoons butter

¾ pound sirloin steak, sliced into
1-inch squares, each ¼ inch
thick

¼ cup coarsely chopped fresh
cilantro

IN A BOWL, stir together ¾ cup of the orange juice, the zest, garlic, salt, and pepper. Set aside.

IN A HEAVY, NONREACTIVE SKILLET over medium-high heat, melt the butter. When it begins to foam, add the beef and sauté for 2 to 3 minutes. Add the orange juice mixture and sauté until cooked to taste, an additional 3 to 4 minutes.

STIR IN half of the cilantro and the remaining ¼ cup orange juice just until mixed. Remove from the heat and serve immediately. Garnish each serving with a little of the remaining cilantro. Serves 4.

Chicken Wings

Covered in a wonderfully sticky glaze,
these are just the way chicken wings should be. Make a triple batch
and cart them off to a picnic in a forest glade or to the beach.
Serve with lots of napkins.

IN A SAUCEPAN over medium heat, warm the oil. Add the garlic and onion and sauté until translucent, about 5 minutes. Stir in the lemon juice, orange juice, sugar, orange zest, Dijon mustard, Worcestershire sauce, dry mustard, brown sugar, vinegar, and salt. Reduce the heat to low and simmer, stirring often, until the sugar dissolves and the sauce begins to thicken to the consistency of warm honey, about 10 minutes. Remove from the heat and let cool to room temperature.

PUT THE CHICKEN WINGS in a large glass or ceramic bowl. Pour the cooled mixture over them, then turn the wings to make sure they are well coated. Let stand for 1 hour or more, turning from time to time. (If allowed to marinate longer than 1 hour, cover and refrigerate.)

PREHEAT an oven to 350 degrees F.

REMOVE THE WINGS from the marinade with a slotted spoon, reserving the marinade, and spread them on an aluminum foil-lined baking sheet. Bake, basting occasionally with the marinade, until the wings are cooked through and slightly crispy, 20 to 30 minutes. Serve the chicken wings hot or cold. Serves 4.

2 tablespoons vegetable oil

2 garlic cloves, finely chopped

$\frac{1}{2}$ cup finely chopped yellow onion

1 tablespoon strained fresh lemon juice

$\frac{1}{2}$ cup strained fresh orange juice (about $1\frac{1}{2}$ oranges)

1 cup sugar

2 tablespoons finely grated orange zest (about 2 oranges)

$\frac{1}{2}$ cup Dijon-style mustard

2 tablespoons Worcestershire sauce

1 tablespoon dry mustard

1 tablespoon brown sugar

2 tablespoons cider vinegar

$\frac{1}{2}$ teaspoon salt

24 chicken wings (about $2\frac{1}{2}$ pounds)

Blood Oranges,

ANCHOVIES, AND SALT-CURED OLIVES

This pleasantly salty salad conjures up images of hot, lazy
evenings along the Mediterranean coast of North Africa, where the scent
of fruit-sweetened rice and couscous dishes perfumes the air.

4 blood oranges

4 to 6 oil-packed anchovy fillets

10 to 12 salt-cured Greek-style

black olives

2 tablespoons extra-virgin olive oil

S L I C E the oranges crosswise into thin rounds, then cut away the rind and remove the seeds. Attractively arrange the orange rounds on a serving dish. Lay the anchovy fillets and olives on top, and then drizzle with the olive oil. Cover with plastic wrap and refrigerate for 5 or 6 hours or overnight.

R E M O V E from the refrigerator about 30 minutes before serving. Serves 4.

Pork Brochettes

New Mexico chilies have a sweet, smoky flavor but carry a fiery kick.
Their complex, intense nature marries well with pork. Take care when handling
the chiles that you do not touch your eyes or other sensitive areas.

2 large dried **New Mexico chili**
    peppers, coarsely chopped,
    stems and seeds removed
¼ cup vegetable oil
1 teaspoon salt
1 teaspoon freshly ground black
    pepper
3 tablespoons fresh thyme
2 tablespoons chopped fresh
    rosemary
½ cup fresh orange juice, including
    pulp (about 1½ oranges)
1 tablespoon red wine vinegar
1½ pounds boneless pork loin,
    trimmed of fat and cut into
    1-inch cubes

P L A C E the dried chilies in a glass or ceramic bowl and stir in the vegetable oil, salt, pepper, thyme, rosemary, orange juice, and vinegar. Add the pork and turn to coat well. Cover and refrigerate for 24 hours, turning from time to time.

I F U S I N G bamboo skewers, soak them in water for 30 minutes and drain before using. Preheat a broiler.

R E M O V E the pork and chili pieces from the marinade with a slotted spoon; discard the marinade. Thread the pork cubes onto the skewers alternately with the chili pieces. Place the skewers on a broiler tray and slip under the broiler about 6 inches from the heat source. Broil on the first side for 5 to 6 minutes. Turn the skewers and broil until cooked through, 3 to 4 minutes longer.

S E R V E the brochettes immediately. Serves 4 to 6.

Salad

OF SWEET ORANGES, ENDIVE, AND SUGARED WALNUTS

Navel oranges are at their best when purchased freshly picked during the months of December and January. Include this crisp salad on your rich winter holiday menus as a palate cleanser following the main course.

TO PREPARE the walnuts, melt the butter in a skillet over high heat. When it begins to foam, add the walnuts and stir until well coated. Reduce the heat to low, add the brown sugar, and stir constantly until the walnuts begin to brown and the sugar starts to caramelize, about 5 minutes. Remove the walnuts to a dish and set aside for 15 to 20 minutes to dry.

IN A SALAD BOWL, whisk together the olive oil, vinegar, and salt and pepper to taste. Add the oranges, endives, and walnuts and toss to distribute the dressing evenly. Serve at once. Serves 4.

2 tablespoons butter

1 cup coarsely chopped walnuts

2 tablespoons brown sugar

1 tablespoon olive oil

1 teaspoon balsamic vinegar

salt and freshly ground black pepper

4 navel or other sweet oranges,
   peeled, sectioned, and cubed

3 heads Belgian endive, cut cross-wise
   into ¼-inch-wide slices

Bread Pudding

This creamy custard with a delicate hint of sweet orange flavor begs
to be served with fresh berries and a swirl of softly whipped cream.
This recipe can be made with any type of sweet orange;
the juice of blood oranges is particularly good.

2 cups milk

2 cups cubed stale white bread,
preferably from a baguette
(1-inch cubes)

3 eggs

½ cup strained fresh orange juice
(about 1½ oranges)

2 tablespoons freshly grated orange
zest (about 2 oranges)

½ cup sugar

1 tablespoon butter

PREHEAT an oven to 400 degrees F.

PLACE the milk in a saucepan over low heat and heat slowly until hot. Do not allow it to boil. Place the bread in a large bowl and pour the hot milk over it; let the bread soak until very soft.

IN A SMALLER BOWL, combine the eggs, orange juice, zest, and sugar. Beat with a whisk until slightly frothy. Fold the egg mixture into the bread-milk mixture. GREASE the bottom and sides of an 8-inch-square glass baking dish with the butter. Pour the bread mixture into the dish, making sure the bread is evenly distributed. Bake until a knife inserted into the center comes out clean, about 45 minutes.

SERVE the bread pudding hot. Serves 6.

Spicy Marinade

WITH ORANGE

This flavorful mixture can be used to baste or marinate a variety of foods. Brush it over swordfish, scallops, chicken, green onions, or thin eggplant rounds for grilling. The acid in the orange juice will "precook" fish and meats slightly, so we suggest marinating them for no more than 1 hour.

COMBINE the orange juice, cayenne pepper, tarragon, and garlic in a small bowl. Mix well. Cover and store for up to 8 hours before using. Makes 1 cup.

1 cup strained fresh orange juice
    (about 3 oranges)
1 teaspoon cayenne pepper or other
    ground dried chili
1 tablespoon minced fresh tarragon
2 garlic cloves, minced
¼ teaspoon salt

Citrus Salsa

This simple salsa is amazingly light and fresh. Sweet orange
combined with sharp lemon strikes a perfect balance, with neither flavor dominating.
Mix this salsa with crème fraîche and spoon the filling into warm crêpes,
or serve alongside a chilled ceviche salad.

1 sweet orange

2 lemons

2 tablespoons pine nuts

2 tablespoons finely chopped
  fresh rosemary

2 tablespoons strained fresh
  lemon juice

1 tablespoon sugar

¼ teaspoon salt

USING a sharp paring knife, peel the zest from the orange and lemons, leaving the white inner rind intact on the fruit. Cut half of the zest into very thin slices, about ¹⁄₁₆ inch wide. Discard the remaining zest or set it aside for another use.

CUT the peeled orange and lemons, with their inner rind intact, into quarters lengthwise. Put the fruit and the pine nuts in a food processor or a blender and process to chop coarsely. Transfer the fruit-nut mixture to a small saucepan and stir in the rosemary, lemon juice, sugar, and salt. Place over medium heat and cook, stirring until the salsa is hot, 3 to 4 minutes.

REMOVE from the heat, stir in the sliced zest, and let cool to room temperature. Spoon into a glass jar, cover tightly, and refrigerate for up to 1 week. Makes about ½ pint.

Custard Tart

OF STRAWBERRIES AND ORANGES

Here, sweet, ripe strawberries from a spring garden are lightly coated in a tangy glaze
of currant jelly and balsamic vinegar and then elegantly laid atop an orange-flavored custard.
Inspired by a classic French strawberry tart, this is an impressive dessert. The custard filling
can be made up to 1 day in advance and refrigerated until the tart is assembled.

For the crust:

1⅓ cups all-purpose flour

2 tablespoons sugar

¼ teaspoon salt

**½ cup (1 stick) unsalted butter,
    chilled and cut into small pieces**

1 to 2 tablespoons ice water

For the filling:

1 cup sugar

5 egg yolks

6 tablespoons all-purpose flour

1 cup heavy cream

1 cup milk

**3 tablespoons freshly grated orange
    zest (about 3 oranges)**

**3 tablespoons strained fresh
    orange juice**

TO MAKE THE CRUST, in a food processor fitted with a metal blade, combine the flour, sugar, and salt. Process briefly to mix. Add the butter and process the mixture until it resembles pea-sized balls. Add the ice water, 1 tablespoon at a time, and process just until the dough forms large, moist clumps. Remove the dough from the food processor, gather into a ball, and then flatten into a disk. Wrap in plastic wrap and chill for 30 minutes. (This dough can also be make by hand by cutting in the butter with a pastry blender or 2 knives and mixing in the ice water with a fork.)

PREHEAT an oven to 350 degrees F. On a lightly floured surface, roll out the dough into a 12-inch round ¼ inch thick. Transfer the round to a 9-inch tart pan with a removable bottom and fit it gently with your fingertips. Trim the edges even with the rim. Line the crust with aluminum foil and fill with dried beans or pie weights. Bake for 15 minutes. Remove the beans or weights and foil, return the crust to the oven, and continue baking until golden brown, about 15 minutes. Transfer the crust to a rack and let cool completely.

TO MAKE THE FILLING, in a large bowl, whisk together the sugar and egg yolks until pale yellow. Whisk in the flour, a little at a time. In a large, heavy saucepan, bring the cream and milk to a boil, remove from the heat and gradually whisk the hot cream mixture into the sugar and egg yolks. Return the mixture to the saucepan and bring to a boil over medium heat, whisking constantly. Reduce the heat to low and continue to cook, whisking constantly until the mixture thickly coats the back of a spoon, about 3 minutes. Pour into a bowl and stir in the orange zest and juice. Press a piece of plastic wrap directly onto the surface of the hot custard to prevent a skin from forming. Refrigerate until cold.

TO MAKE THE GLAZE, combine the jelly, sugar, and vinegar in a small, heavy saucepan and bring to a boil, stirring to dissolve the sugar. Reduce the heat to low and simmer, stirring occasionally, until the mixture coats the back of a spoon, about 2 minutes. Remove from the heat.

PLACE THE HALVED STRAWBERRIES in a bowl and pour the hot glaze over them. Toss to coat well. Let cool for 10 minutes.

SPOON THE FILLING into the crust, smoothing the top. Arrange the halved strawberries, cut sides down, in concentric circles atop the filling. Garnish the center with the 3 whole berries. Sprinkle the orange zest over the tart. Cover and chill until cold, at least 30 minutes but no longer than 2 hours. Serves 8.

For the glaze:

¼ cup red currant jelly

1 tablespoon sugar

1 tablespoon balsamic vinegar
    or red wine vinegar

2 baskets (one pint each)
    strawberries hulled and
    halved lengthwise, plus
    3 whole strawberries, hulled

1 tablespoon minced orange zest
    (about 1 orange)

Savory Galettes

Sweet potatoes are unfairly associated with sticky-sweet holiday side dishes brimming with caramelized marshmallows or canned apricots. These savory orange galettes, a creative mixture of fresh herbs and sweet orange juice, are wonderful crowned with lightly sautéed baby spinach greens.

PREHEAT an oven to 400 degrees F. Using a fork, prick holes in the skin of the sweet potato. Place it on a baking sheet and bake until soft when pierced with a fork, about 1 hour. Remove the sweet potato from the oven. When it is cool enough to handle, peel and discard the skin. Place in a bowl and mash with a fork until smooth. Add the rosemary, garlic, egg, orange juice, and salt, and stir to mix well. Stir in the flour and then the milk, mixing well. The batter should be smooth and thick but not pasty.

HEAT 1 tablespoon of the oil in a large skillet over medium-high heat. Working in batches, spoon in the batter, using 1 heaping tablespoonful to form each galette. Do not crowd the pan. When small bubbles begin to appear on the surface and the first side is golden brown, after about 2 minutes, flip the galettes. Cook until the second side is a rich golden brown, 2 to 3 minutes longer. Remove to a platter and keep warm.

COOK the remaining batter in the same way, adding more oil to the pan as needed to prevent the galettes from sticking. Serve hot. Makes 10 to 12 galettes; serves 4.

1 large sweet potato

2 tablespoons minced fresh rosemary

1 garlic clove, minced

1 egg

1/2 cup strained fresh orange juice
(about 1 1/2 oranges)

1 teaspoon salt

1/2 cup all-purpose flour

1/2 cup milk

About 4 tablespoons light cooking oil

Sherbert

FILLED ORANGES

Citrus trees were popular in the glass greenhouses of fourteenth and fifteenth century France and flourished along the Mediterranean. This is a recipe from the Niçoise area of France, where it is a classic summertime treat for French children. The sherbert-filled oranges and lemons can be bought from roving beach and street vendors. An ice cream maker is needed for these.

16 sweet oranges

2 cups water

2¾ cups sugar

1 tablespoon grated orange zest

2 egg whites

CUT OFF a slice 2 inches in diameter from the stem end of 6 of the oranges. Using a spoon, scoop out the pulp from the oranges, leaving the rinds intact to form shells. Set the pulp, hollowed-out orange shells, and the 2-inch caps in the refrigerator to chill.

JUICE the remaining 10 oranges, then strain the juice. There should be about 4 cups of juice.

IN A SAUCEPAN combine the juice, water, sugar, and zest and bring to a boil over medium high heat. Boil, stirring often for 5 minutes or until the sugar is dissolved. Remove from heat and set aside to cool. While the mixture is cooling, put the egg whites in a medium-size bowl and beat them into stiff peaks using a hand mixer or whisk. Set aside. When the orange mixture is cool, pour it into a large bowl and scoop on the egg whites and gently fold in the egg whites until they are well-blended.

TRANSFER the mixture to an ice cream maker and freeze according to the manufacturer's instructions. When the mixture has begun to harden, stir in the chilled orange pulp and continue to freeze until not fully hardened, but firm. Spoon the sherbert into the orange shells, dividing it evenly and filling them to overflowing. Top with the reserved caps. Freeze the oranges for at least 1 hour, or up to 3 hours, then serve. Serves 6.

Bread Salad

WITH ORANGE AND ARUGULA

*The spicy flavors of arugula and radishes tossed together with
sweet oranges and chunks of savory bread become a celebration of flavor. For a bit
of variety, add lightly sautéed prawns or tender bits of rosemary-roasted chicken.*

¾ cup olive oil

8 slices stale baguette, cut into
    1-inch cubes

¼ cup balsamic vinegar

3 garlic cloves, crushed and then
    minced

½ teaspoon salt

2 large, seedless sweet oranges, such
    as navel, peeled and sectioned

1½ cups small arugula leaves

1 bunch radishes, trimmed and thinly
    sliced (about ½ cup)

HEAT ½ cup of the olive oil in a skillet over medium
heat. Add the bread cubes and sauté, shaking the pan,
until golden on all sides, 4 to 5 minutes. Remove from the
heat and let cool.

IN A LARGE SALAD BOWL, whisk together the
remaining ¼ cup olive oil, the vinegar, garlic, and salt. Cut
the orange sections crosswise into thirds and add them to
the salad bowl, along with the arugula, radishes, and
bread. Toss to distribute the dressing evenly. Serve at
once. Serves 4.

Mandarins

Profiteroles with Mandarin-Cream Filling and Chocolate Sauce *40*

Mandarin Rice with Paprika *42*

Spicy Soup of Mandarin and Coconut *44*

Chicken Salad with Mandarins *46*

$\mathcal{M}$andarins, which are often about the size of golf balls and look like small oranges, are native to China, Indochina, and Japan. There exist many different mandarin varieties, most of which are very sweet and all of which are easy to peel.

The name mandarin was coined during the fruit's journey from China to the West. The same fruit is also known as a tangerine, named for the port of Tangier, Morocco, through which it was distributed to Europe. The clementine, a hybridization of a mandarin with an orange, was created by one Father Clément in Algeria, North Africa. Needless to say, the fruit's interchangeable names have contributed to confusion even among some scientists. Now grown throughout Africa, this orangey-red skinned citrus is valued for its early ripening qualities. In the West African country of Senegal, clementines are frozen and eaten during the late afternoon, beneath the shade of mango and guava trees.

Some other popular mandarin varieties are the Honey mandarin; the early ripening, seedless Japanese Satsuma, grown primarily in Japan and used for canning; and the Fairchild, grown throughout Arizona and California. Because mandarins tend to be sweet, they are excellent substitutes in recipes that call for sweet oranges.

Profiteroles

With each bite of these elegant pastries, the sweet tang of the mandarin and the rich taste of the chocolate meld together, complementing each other. Cream puff pastries are best when served freshly baked, but they can be made several hours ahead, along with the chocolate sauce.

For the pastries:

½ cup boiling water

¼ cup butter

½ cup all-purpose flour

2 eggs

1 egg yolk, lightly beaten

For the filling:

3 tablespoons butter

½ cup sugar

3 egg yolks, lightly beaten

½ cup strained fresh mandarin juice
  (about 2½ mandarins)

1 tablespoon finely grated mandarin
  zest (about 2 mandarins)

1 cup heavy cream

PREHEAT an oven to 425 degrees F.

TO MAKE THE PASTRIES, in a small saucepan, combine the boiling water and the butter. Place the pan over medium heat just until the butter is completely melted. Add the flour all at once and stir vigorously with a wooden spoon until the mixture forms a ball. Remove from the heat and let stand for 5 minutes. Add 1 egg and stir until well blended. Add the second egg and beat again until well blended. The mixture should be stiff, smooth, and shiny. Set aside for 10 minutes to ensure that the batter will set up properly.

USING A TEASPOON, scoop up generous spoonfuls of the dough onto an ungreased baking sheet, forming 1-inch mounds spaced about 2 inches apart. Lightly baste each pastry with the beaten egg yolk. Bake until the pastries are golden brown and have doubled in size, about 20 minutes. Remove from the oven and immediately prick the tops to release the steam. Remove to racks to cool, then cut off the tops to create bowls; reserve the caps.

TO MAKE THE FILLING, in a saucepan over low heat, melt the butter. Add the sugar and egg yolks, and cook, stirring constantly with a wooden spoon, until the sugar dissolves. Stir in the mandarin juice and zest and continue to cook, stirring, until the mixture is thick and does not drip off the back of the spoon, about 15 minutes. Set aside to cool completely.

IN A CHILLED BOWL, whip the cream until it forms stiff peaks. Gently fold the cream into the egg mixture. Cover and chill for 30 minutes.

TO MAKE THE CHOCOLATE SAUCE, in a small saucepan over low heat, melt the butter. Add the chocolate, stirring constantly until it melts, then remove from the heat. Stir in the sugar, mandarin zest, salt, and water and return to low heat. Stir constantly until the sauce has reached the desired thickness and creaminess, 15 to 20 minutes.

TO ASSEMBLE THE PROFITEROLES, spoon generous quantities of the cream filling into the bottom halves of the pastry shells. Top with the caps. Depending on one's love for chocolate, either drizzle or douse the top of each pastry with the warm chocolate sauce. Serve immediately. Makes 12 or 13 pastries; Serves 6.

For the chocolate sauce:

2 tablespoons unsalted butter

2 ounces unsweetened chocolate, chopped

1 cup sugar

1 teaspoon finely grated mandarin zest (about 1 mandarin)

¼ teaspoon salt

½ cup water

Mandarin Rice

WITH PAPRIKA

This rice dish is based on a traditional Hungarian recipe.
The simple combination of paprika, rice, and fresh vegetables suggests
the hearty and flavorful cooking of the spice-filled
kitchens of eastern Europe.

2 cups vegetable or chicken stock

1 cup strained fresh mandarin juice
    (about 5 mandarins)

¾ cup long-grain white rice

¾ cup wild rice

½ cup butter (1 stick)

2 cups chopped celery

2 cups sliced fresh button
    mushrooms

1 cup chopped green onions, in-
    cluding about ⅓ of the tops

1 teaspoon ground cumin

1 teaspoon paprika

1 tablespoon fresh strained lemon
    juice (about ½ lemon)

salt and freshly ground black pepper

½ cup coarsely chopped fresh
    Italian parsley

IN A SAUCEPAN, combine the stock and mandarin juice and bring to a full boil. Add the white rice and wild rice. Reduce the heat to low, cover, and simmer until the rices are tender and the liquid has evaporated, about 40 minutes. The white rice will cook more quickly than the wild rice. When done, the wild rice will be tender, but slightly firmer than the white rice.

MEANWHILE, IN A LARGE SKILLET, melt the butter over medium heat. Add the celery, mushrooms, green onions, cumin, paprika, and lemon juice, salt and pepper. Stir the vegetable mixture so the spices are evenly distributed. Reduce the heat to low, cover, and simmer until the vegetables have cooked down and are stewing in their own juices, about 30 minutes.

IN A LARGE SERVING BOWL, toss together the rice and vegetables. Stir in the parsley and serve immediately. Serves 6.

Spicy Soup

A surprising hint of mandarin finds its way through the spicy, rich flavors of this Southeast Asian coconut soup. Experiment with adding other ingredients, such as shrimp or fresh artichoke hearts. Coconut milk, fish sauce, chili paste, and wood ears can be found in the international food section of grocery stores or in Asian markets.

2 cups water

1 cup long-grain white rice

1 can (14 ounces) coconut milk

1 cup chicken stock

$1/2$ cup strained fresh mandarin juice (about $2^1/2$ mandarins)

1 tablespoon finely grated mandarin zest (about 2 mandarins)

1 tablespoon fish sauce

1 teaspoon Thai chili paste

2 fresh Thai chili peppers, stemmed and seeded (serrano chilies will also work)

2 cups quartered fresh button mushrooms

$1/2$ cup chopped wood ears (fresh or reconstituted)

$1/2$ cup chopped fresh basil

salt and freshly ground black pepper

IN A SAUCEPAN, bring the water to a full boil. Add the rice and boil for 5 minutes. Reduce the heat to low, cover, and cook until tender and the water is absorbed, about 20 minutes.

MEANWHILE, IN A LARGE SAUCEPAN, combine the coconut milk, chicken stock, mandarin juice and zest, fish sauce, chili paste, and chili peppers. Bring to a full boil. Reduce the heat to medium and simmer for about 5 minutes. The stock will be slightly foamy and will have turned a golden-orange color. Add the button mushrooms and wood ears, and cook until the button mushrooms are tender but not mushy, about 5 minutes, but no more than 10 minutes. Remove from the heat and stir in the basil. Season to taste with salt and pepper.

TO SERVE, divide the rice among 6 individual bowls and spoon the soup over the top. Serve immediately. Serves 6.

Chicken Salad

Hot bits of marinated chicken are folded into a tangle of watercress, fresh mint, and mandarin slices to make a main dish salad that zings with distinctive flavors and textures.

4 boneless, skinless chicken breast
halves (about one pound), cut
into large, bite-sized pieces

½ cup plain yogurt

2 tablespoons grated fresh ginger

½ cup fresh mint leaves

2 tablespoons finely grated mandarin
zest (about 3 mandarins)

1 teaspoon ground cumin

1 teaspoon freshly ground black
pepper

4 mandarins

2 cups watercress leaves

1 tablespoon vegetable oil

¼ cup toasted coconut or chopped
almonds (optional)

IN A NONREACTIVE BOWL, stir together the yogurt, ginger, ¼ cup of the mint leaves, mandarin zest, cumin, and black pepper. Cut 1 mandarin in half, squeeze the juice from half of it into the yogurt mixture and mix well. Add the chicken and turn in the marinade evenly, cover, and set aside for 1 hour or refrigerate for up to 12 hours.

PUT THE REMAINING MINT LEAVES and the watercress in another bowl and squeeze in the juice from the remaining mandarin half. Turn the greens to distribute the juice. Peel the remaining mandarins, removing all the white pith, divide them into sections and cut each section in half. Add them to the bowl of greens.

IN A NONSTICK SKILLET over medium heat, warm the vegetable oil. Using a slotted spoon, remove the chicken from the marinade and add to the skillet. Increase the heat to medium-high and cook, stirring often, for 2 to 3 minutes. Pour off the collected juices from the skillet and return it to medium-high heat. Continue to cook the chicken, stirring, until it turns lightly golden, another minute or two.

ADD THE HOT CHICKEN to the bowl of greens and fruit. Toss to mix well. If desired, sprinkle the coconut or almonds over the top. Serve immediately. Serves 3 or 4.

Grapefruits and Pomelos

Escarole Salad with Pomelo and Red Onion *50*

Candied Pomelo Rind *52*

Salad of Warm Grapefruit and Baby Spinach *55*

Breakfast Ham Baked with Brown Sugar Grapefruit *56*

$\mathcal{G}$rapefruits and pomelos are similar in appearance, except for the fact that the latter is nearly twice as large. The pomelo is popular in the Far East, especially in China. It is less juicy than the grapefruit, making it favorable for cooking because it tends to hold its shape better. When cooking pomelos, gently remove the protective membranes from the individual sections first (see Anatomy of Citrus, page 13). The rind of the fruit is commonly candied and can be found in that form in fruitcakes and the French New Year's cake known as *gateau de roi*. Pomelos are often mistakenly sold as grapefruits. Two popular varieties are the pink Chandler and the yellow Reinking.

The sweet-tart flavor of grapefruits, which is not nearly as sour as that of the lemon or lime, works well in savory dishes. A warm grapefruit salad draws the sugar from the fruit, and if cooked over high heat, the sections will begin to caramelize, especially if a teaspoon or so of brown sugar is added. Grapefruits have an extremely high juice content, yielding nearly a cup of juice per fruit. The most readily available varieties are the yellow seedless Marsh and the Red Blush, which has a pinkish tint to its rind and flesh.

Escarole Salad

The name pomelo comes from pamplemousse, *French for grapefruit.*
If pomelos are unavailable, a grapefruit will also work in this simple salad.

2 pomelos

¼ cup finely diced red onion

1 head escarole

For the vinaigrette:

1 tablespoon balsamic vinegar

2 tablespoons extra-virgin olive oil

1 garlic clove, minced

¼ teaspoon salt

PEEL AWAY the outer rind and the soft inner rind from the pomelos. Using a small, sharp paring knife, cut alongside either side of each section to free the sections from the tough membranes encasing them. Place the sections in a bowl, add the red onion, and toss to mix.

REMOVE AND DISCARD the core and the tough outer leaves from the escarole. Arrange the tender inner leaves in a bed on a platter. Spoon the pomelo-onion mixture atop the escarole.

TO MAKE THE VINAIGRETTE, in a small bowl, whisk together the vinegar, olive oil, garlic, and salt. Drizzle the vinaigrette over the salad and serve at once. Serves 6.

Candied Pomelo Rind

Candied citrus rind is an old-fashioned sweet that is worth reviving. Sticks of candied pomelo, dipped in chocolate and served with coffee, make a satisfying end to nearly every meal. Candied pomelo can also be added to fruit salads, muffins, and sweet breads. Use this same process for other citrus rinds, such as orange and lemon.

2 pomelos

4 cups sugar

½ cup light corn syrup

TO PREPARE THE POMELOS, cut each one into quarters from stem to blossom end. Pull the pulp from the rind, leaving the rind pieces intact. Squeeze the fruit juice from the pulp. This should yield 1 cup juice, to use later. Wash the rind and cut it into long ¼-inch-wide strips. Place the rind strips in a large saucepan and add water to cover. Bring to a full boil and cook for 5 minutes. Drain the water off and add fresh water to cover. Bring to a boil and cook the rinds at a full boil for 30 minutes. Drain and pat dry with a dish towel or paper towel. Set aside.

RINSE THE SAUCEPAN. Place the reserved 1 cup pomelo juice, 3 cups of the sugar, and the corn syrup in the pan. Bring the mixture to a slow boil over medium heat, stirring constantly. Add the rind strips to the syrup and cook, stirring occasionally, until the syrup has been fully absorbed and the rind strips are transparent, about 30 minutes. Let cool slightly until they can be handled, about 5 minutes.

LINE A LARGE BAKING SHEET or platter with waxed paper. Place the remaining 1 cup sugar on a large plate and using your fingers, roll the warm rind strips in the sugar, coating evenly. Place on the waxed paper to dry. The rinds will harden slightly and be ready to store after about 1 hour.

TO STORE, transfer to a container with an airtight cover and keep in a cool, dry place for up to 6 months. Makes about 3 cups.

Salad

The tart juices from grapefruit sections make an excellent warm dressing just hot enough to wilt the tender leaves of baby spinach.

IN A SMALL BOWL, whisk together the vinegar, olive oil, and pepper to make a vinaigrette. Set aside.

IN A LARGE, NONREACTIVE SKILLET over a medium-high heat, melt the butter. When the butter begins to foam, add the grapefruit, paprika, and salt. Reduce the heat slightly and sauté until the grapefruit is heated through, 2 to 3 minutes. Add the spinach leaves and gently fold them together with the warm fruit just long enough to wilt the spinach, about 45 seconds.

TRANSFER the warm spinach-grapefruit mixture to a salad bowl and add the vinaigrette. Toss well and divide among 6 individual salad plates. Sprinkle each serving with a little of the cheese and serve immediately.

Serves 6.

1 tablespoon red wine vinegar

2 tablespoons extra-virgin olive oil

1/2 teaspoon freshly ground pepper

1 1/2 teaspoons butter

1 large grapefruit, peeled and
    sectioned, with sections
    cut in half

1 teaspoon paprika

1/2 teaspoon salt

1/2 pound baby spinach leaves

3 tablespoons freshly grated
    romano cheese

Breakfast Ham

BAKED WITH BROWN SUGAR GRAPEFRUIT

*As the brown sugar melts atop the grapefruit slices, it infuses them with
a subtle sweetness that blends well with the sweet-salt taste of the ham.
Add buttered biscuits and glasses of freshly squeezed blood orange juice to
the table for an easy, elegant breakfast.*

2 or 3 grapefruits

1 ham slice, 1 to 1½ pounds and
  ½ inch thick

6 tablespoons firmly packed brown
  sugar

1 tablespoon minced fresh rosemary

PREHEAT an oven to 400 degrees F.

PEEL THE GRAPEFRUITS, removing all the white pith. Cut crosswise into ¼-inch-thick slices.

PUT THE HAM SLICE in a shallow, flameproof dish just large enough to hold it. Cover the ham with the grapefruit slices in a single layer. Place the brown sugar in a sifter or fine-mesh sieve and sift the sugar evenly over the ham slice. Sprinkle the rosemary over the top.

BAKE until the sugar melts and the grapefruit slices are cooked through and are somewhat translucent, 10 to 15 minutes. Then slid the dish under a preheated broiler for 1 to 2 minutes to brown the surface slightly.

REMOVE THE DISH from the broiler and spoon the accumulated juices over the grapefruit slices and ham. Serve hot. Serves 4 to 6.

Kumquats

Kumquats in Brown Sugar and Vanilla Bean Syrup *60*

Bread Stuffing with Kumquats and Grapefruit Juice *61*

Kumquat Curry with Prawns *62*

Chinese Cabbage and Kumquat Salad *64*

*I*n Cantonese, *kumquat* translates as "gold orange," a nod to the fruit's role as a symbol of prosperity. These small, round or oval, orange citrus fruits have semi-sweet rinds and a tart flesh, and the whole fruit is edible. Kumquats are a cultural fixture in their native China, where they are grown on dwarf trees during the Chinese New Year season, to serve as edible holiday decorations. The round Meiwa is less tart than some other varieties and has a very tender outer rind; it is popular in Japan and China. In the United States, the oval and less sweet Nagami kumquat is the most readily available variety. The small fruit trees from the kumquat family make excellent container plants. Large nurseries that carry fruit trees should have dwarf kumquats available, especially during the winter months.

Since kumquats are more tart than sweet, mincing them before adding the fruits to a recipe delivers a subtle presence.

Kumquats

IN BROWN SUGAR AND VANILLA BEAN SYRUP

By cooking kumquats down with sugar and vanilla, the bitterness is removed from the rind and they become a tantalizing garnish or topping for shortcake, ice cream, or such savory dishes as roast pork.

4 cups whole kumquats (25 to 30)

2 cups water

1 cup granulated sugar

1 cup firmly packed brown sugar

1 vanilla bean, cut in half lengthwise

PLACE THE KUMQUATS in a large saucepan and add water to cover. Bring to a full boil and, when foam begins to form on the surface, reduce the heat to medium. Continue to cook for another 10 minutes. Drain the kumquats and set aside.

IN THE SAME SAUCEPAN over a high heat, bring the water to a gentle boil. Add the granulated and brown sugars, reduce the heat to medium, and stir constantly until the sugars have dissolved, about 3 minutes. Add the kumquats and vanilla bean and bring to a full boil. Reduce the heat to low and cook uncovered, stirring occasionally until the kumquats are transparent and soft, about 1 hour. Many of the kumquats will have burst and their skins will appear transparent.

SPOON THE KUMQUATS and syrup into a clean jar, let cool, cover, and refrigerate. They will keep in the refrigerator for up to 2 weeks. Makes about 1 quart.

Bread Stuffing

WITH KUMQUATS AND GRAPEFRUIT JUICE

*Fill a rosemary-seasoned chicken with this tangy stuffing before roasting it,
or bake the stuffing on its own and serve it as a side dish. It is also an irresistible
snack: make a batch in the morning to nibble on throughout the day.*

IN A SKILLET over a medium heat, melt the butter. When it foams, add the onion, garlic, celery, and thyme and sauté until the onion is translucent and the celery is tender, about 10 minutes.

MEANWHILE, COMBINE the grapefruit juice, kumquats, and stock in a saucepan and bring to a boil, and remove from the heat. Place the bread in a bowl and pour the hot liquid over it. Let stand for 5 minutes. Add the sautéed vegetables, egg, parsley, salt and pepper and mix thoroughly.

SPOON THE STUFFING into a 6-pound roasting chicken or 6 Cornish game hens, truss closed, and roast according to your favorite recipe. Or place the stuffing in a small baking dish and bake in an oven preheated to 350 degrees F until the top is golden brown and crunchy, about 15 minutes. Makes about 3 cups; serves 4.

2 tablespoons butter

1 yellow onion, diced

2 garlic cloves, minced

1 cup chopped celery

1 teaspoon minced fresh thyme

$\frac{1}{2}$ cup strained fresh grapefruit juice
(about $\frac{1}{2}$ grapefruit)

2 cups finely chopped kumquats
(about 10 kumquats)

$\frac{1}{2}$ cup vegetable, chicken, or
beef stock

4 cups cubed stale bread,
preferably from a baguette
(1-inch cubes)

1 egg

$\frac{1}{2}$ cup coarsely chopped fresh
parsley

salt and freshly ground black pepper

Kumquat Curry

*Savory dishes cooked with sweet fruits inspire romantic visions of travel
and adventure. Try tossing a tablespoon of freshly grated coconut and a handful
of golden raisins into this creamy citrus curry. Serve with thin slices
of cantaloupe and a potful of saffron rice.*

2 tablespoons butter

1 teaspoon curry powder

2/3 cup heavy cream

2/3 cup water

6 kumquats, minced

3/4 pound large shrimp, peeled and
deveined

IN A LARGE SKILLET over high heat, melt the butter. When it begins to foam, stir in the curry powder and reduce the heat to medium. Cook, stirring, for 2 to 3 minutes. Add the cream, water, and kumquats and cook, continuing to stir, until slightly thickened, about 2 to 3 minutes. Add the shrimp and cook over medium heat until they turn pink and are cooked through, about 3 minutes; do not overcook.

REMOVE FROM THE HEAT and transfer to a warmed serving dish. Serve immediately. Serves 4.

Chinese Cabbage

AND KUMQUAT SALAD

Chinese cabbage, mild and sweet, marries well with the sweet-sharp flavor of kumquats and salty black beans. Look for the nearly white cabbage, also known as napa or celery cabbage, and the salted black beans (commonly packaged in plastic bags) in Asian groceries or well-stocked supermarkets.

1 teaspoon sesame seeds

2 teaspoons light soy sauce

1 tablespoon strained, fresh lemon juice

½ teaspoon sugar

2 cups sliced Chinese cabbage

12 to 15 kumquats, cut crosswise into paper-thin slices

1 tablespoon salted black beans

PUT THE SESAME SEEDS in a small, dry skillet and place over medium heat. Toast them, stirring every 2 to 3 minutes, until lightly golden. Set aside.

IN A SMALL BOWL, whisk together the soy sauce, lemon juice, and sugar to make a dressing. Put the cabbage, kumquats, and black beans in a salad bowl, reserving a few beans and kumquat slices for garnish. Pour the dressing over the salad and turn the leaves to coat evenly. Sprinkle the sesame seeds across the salad and garnish with the reserved kumquat slices and black beans. Serve immediately. Serves 2 or 3.

Lemons and Limes

$\mathcal{A}$lthough lemons and limes immediately bring to mind pitchers of ice-cold summer drinks and fluffy meringue-crowned pies, these tart citrus fruits are actually the secret ingredients of everything from apple chutney to creamy potato soup.

The two most widely available commercial lemon varieties are the Eureka and the Lisbon. But the sweeter Meyer lemon should be sought out. It has a thin, smooth skin and, when fully ripened, is very flavorful and juicy, yielding up to ¾ cup juice per fruit. When a recipe specifies Meyer lemon juice and only more tart varieties are available, add a pinch of sugar for each tablespoon of juice used. Generally, 2½ medium-sized lemons yields ½ cup juice and 4 limes yields ½ cup juice. However, the actual juice yield will vary depending upon the size of the fruits and their individual juice content.

In addition to their roles as major culinary players in heat-beating ades, both lemon and lime juices can serve as flavor substitutes for salt and are regularly used to prevent the discoloration of cut fruits and vegetables. Slice a lemon or lime in half and squeeze the juice over fruit salad or into guacamole, or make a mixture of lemon or lime juice and water for soaking trimmed artichokes or grated celery root.

The two most common lime varieties are the small, yellow-green Mexican lime, which is grown in Mexico and Florida, and the slightly larger, yellowish Bearss lime, which is closely related to, if not the same as, the Persian or Tahiti limes, and grown in California. The Key lime is the same as the Mexican lime but is named after the specific area in which it grows, the Florida Keys. The small, orange Rangpur lime, which is actually a member of the mandarin family, is grouped with limes because of its sour flavor and small size. It can be used in place of lemons or limes in most dishes, and adds a slight orange flavor.

Agua Fresca

*You can omit the ice water and freeze the juice-sugar mixture
in a lock-top freezer bag. Then, to make a festive cocktail, mix the frozen
concentrate with equal parts iced vodka and seltzer water in a blender.
Garnish each serving with freshly crushed mint leaves.*

18 Bearss or Mexican limes

**½ to 1 cup sugar, depending upon
the desired sweetness**

5 cups ice water

THINLY SLICE 2 of the limes crosswise into medallions and set aside. Juice the remaining 16 limes, then strain the juice through a sieve placed over a pitcher to remove the larger bits of pulp and the seeds. You should have about 2 cups juice. Add the sugar and stir until thoroughly dissolved. Add the water and mix well. Toss in the lime slices. Serve cold over crushed ice. Serves 5 or 6.

Chutney

Spoon this versatile sweet chutney over vanilla ice cream,
mix a little into an apple-pie filling, or serve it alongside herb-grilled pork chops.

IN A SAUCEPAN, combine the lime zest and juice, vinegar, and sugar, and heat, stirring, until the sugar dissolves, about 4 minutes. Add the apples, raise the heat to high, and bring to a boil. Reduce the heat to low and cook, uncovered, until the apples are soft and the liquid has reduced to about two-thirds of its original volume, about 45 minutes. Remove from heat and let cool to room temperature.

SPOON THE CHUTNEY into 1 or more clean, dry jars, cover tightly and refrigerate for up to 3 weeks. Makes about 1 quart.

Zest of 3 limes, cut into long strips ⅛ inch wide

1 cup strained fresh lime juice (about 8 limes)

⅓ cup apple cider vinegar

2 cups firmly packed brown sugar

5 large tart green apples, such as Granny Smith or pippin, halved, cored, peeled, and chopped into bite-sized pieces

Potato Soup

WITH MEYER LEMONS

This soup can also be served cold. Cover and refrigerate the puréed soup until well chilled, and then adjust the seasoning before ladling into chilled bowls. Serve with crunchy slices of garlic toast alongside. If you cannot find Meyer lemons, you can substitute Eureka or Lisbon lemons.

2 tablespoons butter

2 yellow onions, thinly sliced

1 tablespoon finely grated lemon zest
(about 2 lemons)

1/2 teaspoon grated, peeled fresh
ginger

1 cup strained fresh lemon juice,
preferably Meyer lemon

1/2 teaspoon sugar, if using Eureka or
Lisbon lemon juice, mixed with
the lemon juice

1/2 teaspoon salt

1/2 teaspoon freshly ground black
pepper

4 cups water

4 large red potatoes, peeled and
boiled until tender, then
coarsely chopped

2 tablespoons finely chopped fresh
Italian parsley

IN A SAUCEPAN over a medium heat, melt the butter. When it begins to foam, add the onions, lemon zest, and ginger and sauté until the onions are translucent, about 10 minutes. Add the lemon juice (with the sugar, if using), salt, and pepper; continue to sauté for 2 to 3 minutes longer. Add the water, raise the heat to high, and bring to a boil. Cover, reduce the heat to medium, and simmer until the broth is golden and the onions have almost disintegrated, about 30 minutes.

REMOVE from the heat and strain through a sieve into a clean container; discard the contents of the sieve. Working in batches, if necessary, combine the strained stock and the potatoes in a blender or food processor and purée until smooth. Transfer the purée to a clean saucepan and bring to a gentle boil.

LADLE into warmed soup bowls and garnish each serving with a little of the parsley. Serves 4.

POTATO

Artichokes

STUFFED WITH GROUND LAMB AND LEMON

*Lamb, like feta cheese, eggplants, and grape leaves, resonates
with the aromas and flavors of Greek cooking. Here, ground lamb is seasoned
with lemon juice before being stuffed into hollowed artichokes and baked.*

4 large artichokes

2 quarts water plus ¼ cup
strained fresh lemon juice
(about 1½ lemons)

4 or 5 slices stale bread, preferably
from a baguette

1 cup water

½ pound lean ground lamb

1 egg

1 teaspoon salt

1 teaspoon freshly ground black
pepper

2 tablespoons minced fresh oregano

1 tablespoon minced fresh chives

½ cup strained fresh lemon juice
(about 2½ lemons)

2 tablespoons olive oil

4 thin lemon slices

PREHEAT an oven to 350 degrees F.

TO PREPARE THE ARTICHOKES, working with
1 artichoke at a time, snap or cut off any tough or
bruised outer leaves. Cut off about one-third of the tops
and cut off the stem even with the bottom. Using a small
spoon, scoop out the center, removing all of the choke
and thistles.

IN A LARGE POT, bring the mixture of water and
lemon juice to a boil. Add the artichokes and cook until
slightly tender, about 15 minutes. Using tongs, remove
the artichokes and drain, upside down, for 10 minutes or
longer.

LAY THE BREAD SLICES in a shallow bowl and
add the 1 cup water. Let soak until fully softened, 10 to
15 minutes. Using your hands, squeeze the moisture
out of the bread and then place the bread in a mixing
bowl. Add the lamb, egg, salt, pepper, oregano, chives, and
¼ cup of the lemon juice. Stir well to make a thick paste.

WORKING with 1 artichoke at a time, gently pull back
the leaves row by row and tuck a bit of the filling near the
base of each leaf. Fill the center of each artichoke with a
mound of the filling.

OIL THE BOTTOM AND SIDES of a baking dish just large enough to hold the artichokes in a single layer with 1 tablespoon of the olive oil. Pour the remaining 1 tablespoon olive oil and ¼ cup lemon juice into the bottom of the dish, then stand the artichokes upright in the dish. Place a lemon slice atop each artichoke.

BAKE, BASTING OFTEN with the juices in the dish, until the stuffing is cooked through, the artichokes are tender, and the tops are crunchy, about 30 minutes. If desired, run the artichokes under the broiler for 2 or 3 minutes to brown the tops. Serve hot or at room temperature. Serves 4.

Celery Root Slaw

WITH CUMIN-LEMON DRESSING

*Celery root is a versatile vegetable that is too often overlooked.
Its earthy flavor and firm texture are nicely balanced by a lemony cumin dressing
in this refreshing change from shredded cabbage or carrot slaw. There is no need to
add sugar to the lemon juice in this recipe if not using Meyer lemons.*

½ cup strained fresh lemon juice
(about 1 Meyer or 2½ Lisbon
or Eureka lemons)

1 teaspoon ground cumin

⅛ teaspoon ground turmeric

⅛ teaspoon salt

¼ teaspoon freshly ground black
pepper

2 tablespoons minced fresh parsley

1 celery root (about ½ pound)

IN A SALAD BOWL, stir together the lemon juice, cumin, turmeric, salt, pepper, and parsley, until well blended.

PEEL THE CELERY ROOT and cut it into thin strips about 1/16 inch wide and 2 inches long. Add the celery root to the dressing and toss to coat well. Serve at once. Serves 4.

Poached Fish

A spicy-sweet salsa made from perfumed papaya, sour Seville orange juice, and refreshingly tart lime juice colorfully crowns delicately seasoned sautéed fish. If sour oranges are unavailable, use equal parts orange and lemon juice.

IN A BOWL, stir together the papayas, tomatillos, chilies, salt, and lime juice. Let stand at room temperature. IN A LARGE NONSTICK SKILLET over medium heat, combine the butter and vegetable oil. When the butter foams, toss in the cumin and cayenne or other chili and stir for a second or two until the spices are fragrant. Add the fish and cook over medium heat, turning once, for 2 or 3 minutes on each side. Add the orange juice and water, cover, and cook over low heat until the fish flakes easily, 5 minutes longer.

REMOVE THE FISH FILLETS to individual plates and pour some of the pan juices over each serving. Top each serving with 1 or 2 tablespoonfuls of the salsa. Serve any remaining salsa in a small bowl along with the fish. Serves 4.

3 papayas, halved, seeded, peeled, and cut into ¼-inch cubes

6 tomatillos, papery husks removed, finely chopped

6 fresh serrano chili peppers, stemmed, seeded, and minced

⅛ teaspoon salt

¼ cup strained fresh lime juice (about 2 limes)

1 tablespoon butter

1 tablespoon vegetable oil

¼ teaspoon ground cumin

½ teaspoon ground cayenne or other pure ground chili

4 firm fish fillets, such as sea bass, salmon, or halibut, each about 6 to 8 ounces and ½ inch thick

¼ cup fresh Seville or other sour orange juice (about 1 orange)

¼ cup water

Salmon

PAN-GRILLED WITH LEMON DEGLAZE

The salmon fillets are quickly seared, which releases their natural juices
to mingle delectably with the chili, lemon juice, and white wine.

1 teaspoon butter

2 skinless salmon fillets, about
    6 to 8 ounces each

¼ teaspoon salt

½ teaspoon ground cayenne or other
    pure ground chili

½ cup strained fresh lemon juice,
    preferably Meyer lemon (about
    1 Meyer lemon or 2½ Lisbon
    or Eureka lemons)

¼ teaspoon sugar, if using Lisbon or
    Eureka lemon juice, mixed with
    the lemon juice

¼ cup dry white wine

IN A SMALL SKILLET, preferably nonstick, over medium-high heat, melt the butter. Add the salmon fillets and sear 1 to 2 minutes on each side.

SPRINKLE THE FILLETS with the salt and cayenne or other chili. Add the lemon juice (with the sugar if using) and the wine. Reduce the heat to low, cover, and cook until the salmon flakes easily, 2 to 3 minutes. Serve immediately on individual plates. Serves 2.

Rangpur

Although the Rangpur lime is not a true lime, its tart flavor allows for its use in recipes that call for lemons or limes. The juice squeezed from its deep orange pulp lightly colors this traditional lemon curd with a slight tinge of orange. Spread the curd onto freshly baked scones or butter cookies, or eat it right out of the jar.

IN THE TOP PAN of a double boiler, combine the egg yolks and sugar. Place over the lower pan of gently simmering water. Do not allow the water to boil. Using a whisk, beat the yolks and sugar together until the mixture becomes creamy and pale and forms thin strands when dropped from the edge of a spoon, about 4 minutes.

BEAT IN THE LIME JUICE and zest, and then gradually add the butter slices while stirring constantly. Continue cooking, stirring constantly, until the mixture begins to thicken, about 20 minutes. Be careful that the mixture does not boil.

WHILE THE CURD IS STILL HOT, spoon it into 1 or more clean, dry jars and cap tightly. Allow to cool and then refrigerate. It will keep in the refrigerator for up to a week. Makes 1 pint.

6 egg yolks

1 cup superfine sugar

¾ cup strained fresh Rangpur lime juice (about 7 limes)

2 tablespoons finely grated Rangpur lime zest (4 or 5 Rangpur limes)

½ cup unsalted butter, at room temperature, cut into ½-inch-thick slices

Lemon

BUTTER COOKIES

*These simple cookies are made from creamy lemon batter speckled throughout
with vanilla bean flecks. Substitute mandarin, lime, or orange zest for the lemon zest
to change the color and the flavor. If you have no vanilla bean, ¹/₂ teaspoon
of pure vanilla extract will work.*

²/₃ cup butter, at room temperature

2 tablespoons finely grated lemon
    zest (about 4 lemons)

¹/₂ cup granulated sugar

1 egg

1 vanilla bean

2¹/₄ cups all-purpose flour

¹/₄ cup confectioners sugar for
    dusting

IN A MIXING BOWL, cream the butter with the back of a fork until it is smooth, about 5 minutes. Add the lemon zest and continue to blend until well mixed. Add the granulated sugar and mix until smooth, 2 minutes longer. Add the egg and beat vigorously until a smooth lemony-yellow batter forms, another 5 minutes.

SLIT THE VANILLA BEAN in half lengthwise. Using the tip of a sharp knife, scrape the tiny seeds into the batter and then stir to distribute evenly. Slowly stir in 2 cups of the flour, and mix until the dough comes together, pulls away from the sides of the bowl, and a ball forms. Remove from the bowl, flatten into a small disk, and wrap in plastic or foil wrap. Chill for 15 minutes.

PREHEAT an oven to 375 degrees F.

GENEROUSLY FLOUR a dry flat surface and a rolling pin with part of the remaining ¼ cup flour. Remove the dough from the refrigerator and roll it out onto a ¼-inch-thick sheet. Using a round cookie cutter 2 inches (5 cm) in diameter, cut out cookies and transfer them to an ungreased baking sheet, about ¾ inch apart. Gather up the scraps, apply more flour to the work surface and rolling pin, and roll them out. Continue to cut out cookies until no dough remains.

BAKE until a golden brown edge appears around each cookie, 7 or 8 minutes. Remove from the oven and transfer to a wire rack. Let cool completely, about 30 minutes, then lightly dust with confectioners sugar. Store in an airtight container at room temperature for up to 1 week. Makes about 3 dozen cookies.

Index

    Breakfast Ham Baked with Brown Sugar Grapefruit *56*

    Chicken Wings with Orange-Mustard Glaze *21*

    Kumquat Curry with Prawns *62*

    Mandarin Rice with Paprika *42*

    Poached Fish with Papaya and Tomatillo Salsa *75*

    Pork Brochettes Marinated in Orange Sauce *24*

    Salmon Pan-Grilled with Lemon Deglaze *76*

    Sirloin Strips Sautéed with Orange Juice *20*

Mandarin Rice with Paprika *42*

Poached Fish with Papaya and Tomatillo Salsa *75*

Pork Brochettes Marinated in Orange Sauce *24*

Potato Soup with Meyer Lemons *70*

Profiteroles with Mandarin-Cream Filling and Chocolate Sauce *40*

Rangpur Lime Curd *77*

Salad of Sweet Oranges, Endive, and Sugared Walnuts *25*

Salad of Warm Grapefruit and Baby Spinach *55*

Salads:

    Blood Oranges, Anchovies, and Salt-Cured Olives *22*

    Bread Salad with Orange and Arugula *36*

    Celery Root Slaw with Cumin-Lemon Dressing *74*

    Chicken Salad with Mandarins *46*

    Chinese Cabbage and Kumquat Salad *64*

    Escarole Salad with Pomelo and Red Onion *50*

    Salad of Sweet Oranges, Endive, and Sugared Walnuts *25*

    Salad of Warm Grapefruit and Baby Spinach *55*

Salmon Pan-Grilled with Lemon Deglaze *76*

Savory Galettes of Sweet Potato and Orange *33*

Sherbert-Filled Oranges *34*

Side dishes:

    Mandarin Rice with Paprika *42*

    Savory Galettes of Sweet Potato and Orange *33*

Sirloin Strips Sautéed with Orange Juice *20*

Soups:

    Potato Soup with Meyer Lemons *70*

    Spicy Soup of Mandarin and Coconut *44*

Spicy Marinade with Orange *27*

Spicy Soup of Mandarin and Coconut *44*

Table of Equivalents

The exact equivalents in the following tables have been rounded for convenience.

US/UK

oz=ounce
lb=pound
in=inch
ft=foot
tbl=tablespoon
fl oz=fluid ounce
qt=quart

METRIC

g=gram
kg=kilogram
mm=millimeter
cm=centimeter
ml=milliliter
l=liter

Liquids

US	METRIC	UK
2 tbl	30 ml	1 fl oz
1/4 cup	60 ml	2 fl oz
1/3 cup	80 ml	3 fl oz
1/2 cup	125 ml	4 fl oz
2/3 cup	160 ml	5 fl oz
3/4 cup	180 ml	6 fl oz
1 cup	250 ml	8 fl oz
1 1/2 cups	375 ml	12 fl oz
2 cups	500 ml	16 fl oz
4 cups/1 qt	1 l	32 fl oz

Oven Temperatures

FAHRENHEIT	CELSIUS	GAS
250	120	½
275	140	1
300	150	2
325	160	3
350	180	4
375	190	5
400	200	6
425	220	7
450	230	8
475	240	9
500	260	10

Weights

US/UK	METRIC
1 oz	30 g
2 oz	60 g
3 oz	90 g
4 oz (1/4 lb)	125 g
5 oz (1/3 lb)	155 g
6 oz	185 g
7 oz	220 g
8 oz (1/2 lb)	250 g
10 oz	315 g
12 oz (3/4 lb)	375 g
14 oz	440 g
16 oz (1 lb)	500 g